A JOURNEY IN COLOR

THE ART OF ELLIS WILSON

Written by

Jayne Moore Waldrop *Jayne Moore Waldrop 2022*

Illustrated by

Michael McBride

Shadelandhouse
MODERN PRESS

Lexington, Kentucky

*Dedicated to the memory and artistic legacy of Ellis Wilson (1899–1977)
and to all who follow their dreams*

I discovered Ellis Wilson's remarkable art through the work of Albert Sperath, former curator at the Clara M. Eagle Gallery at Murray State University in Murray, Kentucky. After arriving at Murray State, Sperath noticed two Wilson paintings in the permanent collection and learned that Wilson had been born in nearby Mayfield, Kentucky. Sperath tracked down Wilson's paintings in museums and private collections to organize a retrospective exhibit that opened in 2000. Together, Sperath, Margaret R. Vendryes, Steven H. Jones, and Eva King wrote *The Art of Ellis Wilson* (University Press of Kentucky, 2000). Kentucky Educational Television (KET) produced a companion documentary called *Ellis Wilson—So Much to Paint*. Their work inspired me to learn more. In 2009, I wrote about Wilson for *Kentucky Monthly* magazine and included quotes from Sperath. I also began working on this book because, if I've learned anything from studying Ellis Wilson's life, it's to not give up on a dream. I reviewed Wilson's papers housed at the Smithsonian Institution's Archives of American Art, read his interviews, and most importantly, looked at his art.

I deeply appreciate the support of authors George Ella Lyon and DaMaris B. Hill, who read earlier versions of the manuscript and encouraged me to keep working. To Shadelandhouse Modern Press, thank you for believing in this book. Thanks to Virginia Underwood for her meticulous care and expertise in publishing and to Michael McBride for creating the beautiful illustrations that complete this telling of Ellis Wilson's story for a new generation.

A Shadelandhouse Modern Press book for young readers
A Journey in Color: The Art of Ellis Wilson

Text Copyright © 2022 Jayne Moore Waldrop
Illustrations Copyright © 2022 Michael McBride

**Shadelandhouse, Shadelandhouse Modern Press,
and the colophon are trademarks of Shadelandhouse Modern Press, LLC.
All rights reserved.
Printed in Canada
For information about permissions, please direct inquiries:
Permissions, Shadelandhouse Modern Press, LLC
P.O. Box 910913
Lexington, KY 40591
or email permissions@smpbooks.com.**

**Published in the United States of America by:
Shadelandhouse Modern Press, LLC, Lexington, Kentucky
smpbooks.com**

**First edition 2022
Library of Congress Control Number: 2022946384
ISBN: 978-1-945049-34-7 (Hardcover)**

**Illustrations by: Michael McBride
Cover and book design: Brooke Lee**

At a time when most folks saw the world as black or white,

young Ellis Wilson watched colors dance across canvas.

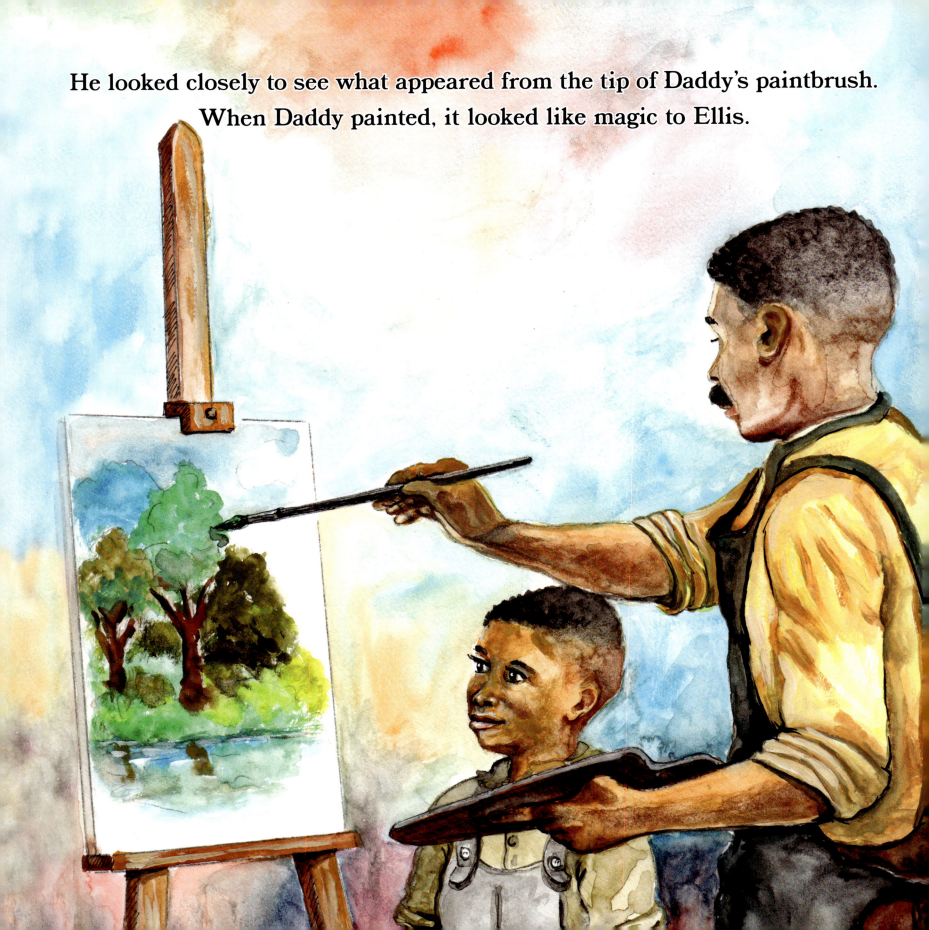

He looked closely to see what appeared from the tip of Daddy's paintbrush. When Daddy painted, it looked like magic to Ellis.

"When I grow up, I want to paint...

all the time," Ellis said.

"Son, a man can't make a living like this. Let's go to work."

They walked through town to a tiny barbershop.

Witch hazel and shaving soap scented the air.

Their side of the creek was known as the Bottom, and Ellis Wilson's family had lived there all his life.

As Ellis swept the floor,
he listened to the men laugh
and tell stories.

He settled into a chair to watch
Daddy's hands move expertly
around each head,
           snipping here,
clipping there.

With a tiny piece of soap
and a scrap of pasteboard,
he drew what he saw.

"Ellis, you learning to cut hair?"
the man in the chair asked.

"No, sir. I'm going to be an artist,"
Ellis said.

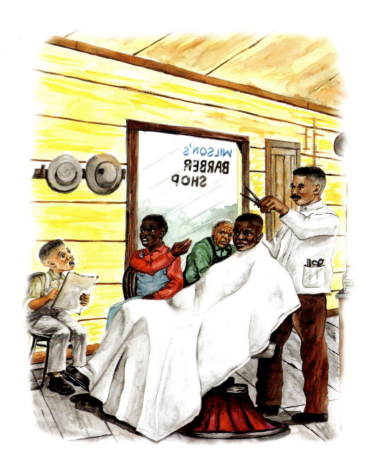

The men just shook their heads. Ellis Wilson didn't look like an artist. He came from a small town in Kentucky not known for artists, especially on this side of the creek.

"Now that's a crazy notion," the man said.

"If you want to be a painter, come paint my shed," said another.

The men chuckled, but Ellis kept drawing.

At church, Ellis watched the choir ladies practice their songs while he waited for his mother. He sketched what he saw.

He heard Mama telling the others that he'd soon go to college, the first in their family.

"Will you study teaching or farming?" asked one of the women.

"No, ma'am. I'm going to be an artist," Ellis said.

"Why you'll starve to death!" said another.

The ladies nodded.

He didn't want to be a farmer, a barber, or a teacher.

He wanted to be an artist.

He wanted to make colors dance across canvas.

He dreamed of seeing a world appear from the tip of *his* paintbrush.

He wanted to study art.

Ellis knew that most art schools only taught white students, but he didn't give up.

He applied for admission.

The schools said *No*.

He sent examples of his best art.

The schools said *No*.

Sometimes it felt like the whole world was saying *No*.

Finally, one school saw his talent and said *Yes*.

He boarded the all-night train bound for Chicago,

a city full of lights, crowds, smokestacks, and noise.

The place was nothing like the Bottom.

But Ellis decided to stay.

Don't worry about me, he told his family in a letter. *This is where I belong.*

In class, Ellis painted flowers, models, and landscapes.
He studied to understand form, color, and line.

Colors began to dance across his canvas. From the tip of Ellis's paintbrush,
the world that appeared looked different and full of change.

He headed to New York City,

a place well known for art and artists.

In his Harlem neighborhood, Ellis met

other painters,

    sculptors,

        musicians,

            poets,

        and dancers.

There is so much to paint and so little time, he wrote to his family.

Into the envelope he slipped newspaper clippings. A headline read

Ellis Wilson Wins Fine Art Prize

He lived alone in a small apartment, nothing fancy.

Life as an artist wasn't easy, but it was the life Ellis wanted.

He worked odd jobs to pay the rent and put food on the table.

He worked as a museum guard, a handyman, and sometimes a messenger.

And Ellis kept painting.

As he went about his day, he studied people.

He sketched what he saw and made notes,

putting colors into words to help him remember.

After work he went home and painted.

      The world as Ellis saw it,

         bold colors,

           simple shapes,

              the people and their hopes,

                had not been painted before.

From the streets and from his travels, he painted ordinary folks.
People working and living their lives.

Assembly-line workers building cars and airplanes.

Women strolling with their babies.

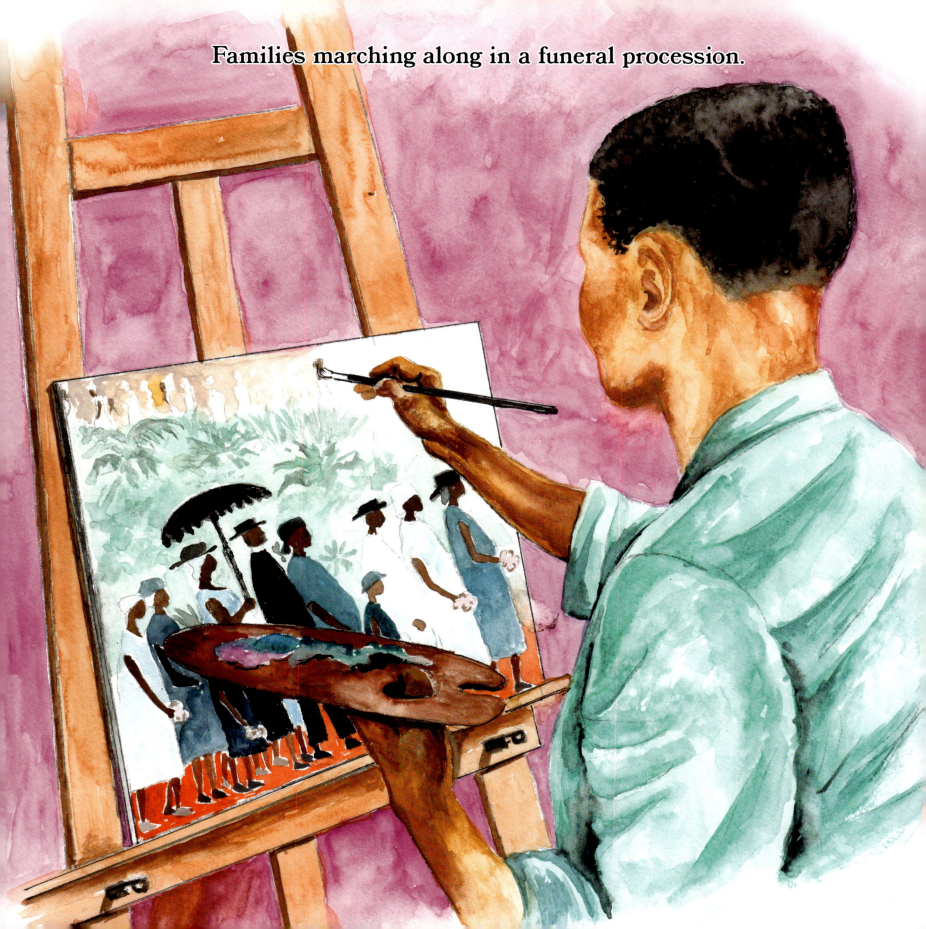
Families marching along in a funeral procession.

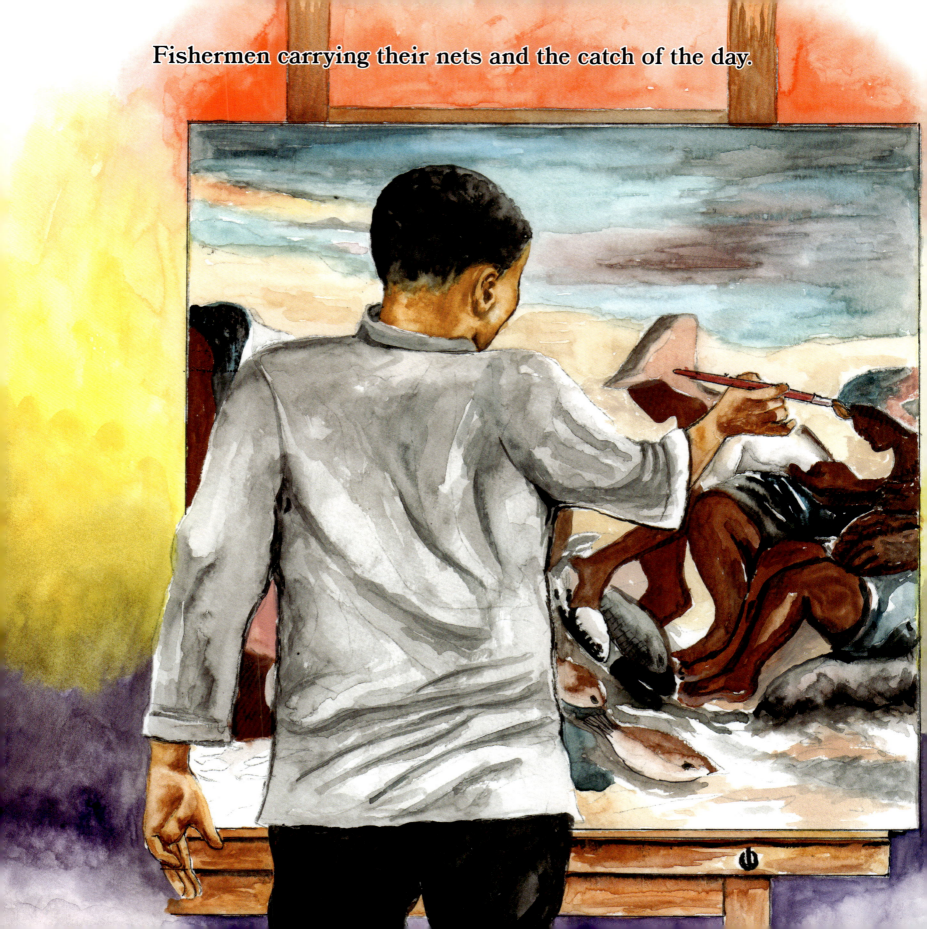
Fishermen carrying their nets and the catch of the day.

From the tip of Ellis Wilson's paintbrush a world appeared, and it was filled with color and magic for everyone to see.

Author's Note

ELLIS WILSON was born in 1899 in Mayfield, Kentucky. He grew up in the Bottom, the town's African American section during racial segregation. His father ran a successful barbershop and was a self-taught artist who took a few lessons from an itinerant painter. His mother worked as a housekeeper. Wilson credited his father as his inspiration to paint and his mother for motivating him to get an education.

Because of segregation laws, few art schools accepted African American students, regardless of their artistic talents. Eventually, he was admitted to the prestigious Art Institute of Chicago. After completing his degree, he moved to New York City and became part of the flourishing arts community of the Harlem Renaissance during the 1920s. In 1944, his work achieved major recognition when he became one of the first African American artists to be awarded a Guggenheim Foundation fellowship. He applied for the fellowship four times before winning the honor. Again, Wilson didn't give up on his dream. In his Guggenheim application, he described his plans for the fellowship: "I want to paint all the time—everything of interest and beauty... So much to paint and so little time."

During his life, his art was shown in many galleries and museums in New York, Washington, DC, and Chicago, but he once said that the exhibitions of his paintings back home in western Kentucky were the highlights of his career. Despite critical acclaim for his art, he died in poverty in 1977. Today, Ellis Wilson's vibrant work hangs in many art museums and private collections.

JAYNE MOORE WALDROP is a writer and attorney who loves telling stories about her native western Kentucky. She is the author of *Drowned Town* (University Press of Kentucky, 2021), an INDIES Book of the Year Award silver winner in fiction, and of *Retracing My Steps* (2019) and *Pandemic Lent: A Season in Poems* (2021), both published by Finishing Line Press. This is her debut children's book.

MICHAEL MCBRIDE, a Nashville, Tennessee-based artist and a professor at Tennessee State University, has illustrated over 75 children's books. He was featured in *Visions of My People: Sixty Years of African American Art in Tennessee*, an exhibit organized by the Tennessee State Museum. He was commissioned to paint a four-story mural honoring US Representative John Lewis, completed and installed in downtown Nashville in November 2021. *Too Black Too Fast* is a touring art exhibit created by McBride to celebrate the history of African American jockeys in Thoroughbred racing and their contributions to the sport. McBride earned his undergraduate degree in art from Tennessee State University and his graduate degree in painting from Illinois State University.